PREPARATION FOR RESOLUTION

God's Wisdom for Resolving Conflict

Lester Adams

Preparation for Resolution by Lester L. Adams

No part of this book may be reproduced in any form, stored in a retrieval system, or transmitted in any form by any means—electronic, mechanical, photocopy, recording, or otherwise—without prior written permission of the publisher, except as permitted by US copyright law.

Unless otherwise noted, Scripture quotations are from the King James Version of the Bible. Wherever *Strong's Concordance* is mentioned, it refers to *The New Strong's Exhaustive Concordance of the Bible*, by James Strong, copyright © 1990 by Thomas Nelson Publishers.

Copyright 2014 by Lester L. Adams
All rights reserved.

ISBN: 0984967842
ISBN 13:9780984967841

Pursuing Peace Publishing and Ministries
www.pursuingpeaceministry.org

Adams, Lester L.
Preparation for Resolution
E-book ISBN:

Contents

ACKNOWLEDGEMENTS	v
INTRODUCTION	vii
CHAPTER 1: Trust God	1
CHAPTER 2: Seek God	9
CHAPTER 3: Pray for God's Will	17
CHAPTER 4: Pray for Each Other	21
CHAPTER 5: Tackle Repeated Conflict	27
CHAPTER 6: Engage in Discussion	33
CHAPTER 7: Identify Major and Minor Issues	39
CHAPTER 8: Speak in Gentle Tones	43
CHAPTER 9: Have the Right Facts	51
CHAPTER 10: Hear Each Other	57
CHAPTER 11: Confess Your Faults	63
CHAPTER 12: End Conflict	69
CHAPTER 13: Forgive Each Other	75
CHAPTER 14: Reconcile	81
CONCLUSION	89
RESOURCES	91
ABOUT THE AUTHOR	93

Acknowledgements

My deepest appreciation to...

My wife, Jill- Thank you for your support, and your steadfastness in seeking the Lord for the two of us to be one.

Pastor Thomas Schwind and First Lady Rosalind Schwind- Thank you for your prayers and support. My sincere appreciation for our friendship and relationship.

My cousin, Anthony Adams- Thank you for your insightful guidance

Everyone who prayed for me during the twenty years it took to complete this work. Thank you and may God richly bless you

Most of all, I want to thank Jesus Christ my Lord and Savior, who made this all possible. I can hardly believe that God chose me, a person who types with one finger, to author so many articles and now books. To God be the glory!

Introduction

And he shall go before him in the spirit and power of Elijah, to turn the hearts of the fathers to the children, and the disobedient to the wisdom of the just; to make ready a people prepared for the Lord.
—Luke 1:17

Many people have a difficult time dealing with conflict. Over the past twenty years, I've had the privilege of helping people resolve their differences. I've mediated numerous conflicts in my law practice, my mediation ministry, my role as a church elder, and as a mediator who has facilitated discussions for various conflict-resolution organizations.

The conflicts I've been involved with cover many different areas and have included sibling rivalries, family disputes, children-parent disagreements, rifts between church leaders, multimillion-dollar stockholder disputes, employment and racial-discrimination grievances, disagreements between neighbors, and accusations of treachery and deceit between business partners.

I also have written a number of articles on congregational conflict resolution that have been disseminated and read throughout the United States and in countries such as Israel, Germany, Ireland, Kenya, the Philippines, and Spain. People who read my articles often contact me, asking permission to use my written materials or seeking counsel regarding how to resolve conflict. As a result I've had the pleasure of communicating with people both near and far away regarding the subject of making peace.

Preparation for Resolution

The requests for help have been increasing. Because many people struggle with resolving conflict and because I love to see people find peace with each other, I wrote *Preparation for Resolution* to give people guidance on using the Scriptures to resolve conflict.

In my experience one of the main reasons people have difficulty resolving conflict is because *they do not use God's word to settle their differences.* Some people encourage others to use the Scriptures to resolve their conflict, but when they themselves are in conflict, they disregard the Scriptures they advise others to use. God gave us his word to give us solutions to our problems.

> Thy word is a lamp unto my feet; and a light unto my path. (Psalm 119:105)

> All Scripture is given by inspiration of God, and is profitable for doctrine, for reproof, for correction, for instruction in righteousness: That the man of God may be perfect, thoroughly furnished unto all good works. (2 Timothy 3:16–17)

When I told a good friend that God had called me to help people resolve conflict, he said, "You know, chapter eighteen, verse fifteen of the Book of Matthew is one of the most disregarded passages in the Scriptures."

> Moreover if thy brother shall trespass against thee, go and tell him his fault between thee and him alone; if he shall hear thee, thou hast gained thy brother. (Matthew 18: 15)

In my experience his words ring true. I often have witnessed church leaders who know God's word (and preach it every week) totally disregard this Scripture and other Scriptures when they become engaged in conflict with each other.

As long as we reject the counsel of God's word or live by the motto "Do as I say, not as I do," we won't get the help from God we need to resolve our disputes.

Introduction

Part of our problem today is that we do not love the word of God. If we did, we would receive God's word with gladness and begin to apply it immediately in our lives as the children of our church did when I taught them Biblical conflict resolution at a summer camp we held in 2011. It was a joy to teach them because they were so receptive to God's word. If we start applying God's word with the same exuberance and zeal as these children did, God will give us the help we need. And we will be much, more effective in resolving our conflict.

> Great peace have they which love thy law: and nothing shall offend them (Psalm 119: 165)

Instead of having our children lead us by example, we, who are adults and leaders in the church should be leading our children by example and raising up a generation of peacemakers who love God and walk in his ways.

Many people are unable to settle their disputes because *they're unprepared to do so*. People who aren't ready for discussion get very little done; as a result they remain in conflict when they could have resolved their disagreement if they had been properly prepared for discussion.

One of the goals of *Preparation for Resolution* is to discuss the subject of people's hearts, to help make individuals spiritually prepared to more effectively resolve their differences. When we are prepared in this manner, we allow God to release his power to help us settle our differences.

God told Joshua we can gain such success when we walk in the guidance we receive from God's word.

> This book of the law shall not depart out of thy mouth, but thou shalt meditate therein day and night, that thou mayest observe to do according to all that is written therein: for then thou shalt make thy way prosperous, and then thou shalt have good success. (Joshua 1:8)

God's conflict-resolution principles work because God releases his power to help us resolve our conflicts.

> When a man's ways please the Lord, he makes even his enemies be at peace with him. (Proverbs 16:7)

I have seen these principles work in my life and relationships, as well as in the lives of others in conflict who choose to walk in them. I encourage you to read this book slowly and pray as you read its many Scriptures so that God can touch your heart and give you the greater understanding you need to resolve your disagreements.

CHAPTER 1

TRUST GOD

God is our refuge and our strength, a very present help in trouble.
—Psalm 46:1

Proverbs 3:5 states "Trust in the Lord with all your heart." According to *Strong's Concordance*, the Hebrew word for trust is *batach* (pronounced "baw-takh"). It means to trust, be confident in, or be sure. To be effective in resolving conflict, we must put our trust in God instead of in ourselves or other people.

We can trust God to help us settle our differences because *he has the power to do so*. Psalm 76:1–3 reveals how great God's power is to end conflict.

> In Judah is God known: his name is great in Israel. In Salem also is his tabernacle, and his dwelling place in Zion. There brake he the arrows of the bow, the shield, and the sword, and the battle.

Some of the weapons we use against each other are harsh, unkind, and destructive words that flow out of our hearts. These words pierce and cut others as swords and spears do to hurt our human bodies.

> The tongue deviseth mischiefs; like a sharp razor, working deceitfully (Psalm 52: 2).

> The words of his mouth were smoother than butter, but war was in his heart: his words were softer than oil, yet they were drawn swords (Psalm 55: 21)

> My soul is among lions: and I lie even among them that are set on fire, even the sons of men, whose teeth are spears and arrows, and their tongue a sharp sword (Psalm 57: 4)

The way that God breaks these weapons is to deal with our hearts about the things in us that cause us to start conflict and do destructive things to each other. The fact that God breaks the weapons we use to fight each other shows his awesome strength and might. This passage also makes it clear that God has the ability to end our conflict. Psalm 46:9 confirms God's power to end our disputes.

> Come behold the works of the Lord, who has made desolations in the earth. He maketh wars to cease unto the ends of the earth; He breaks the bow and cuts the spear in two. He burns the chariots in the fire.

This passage provides other descriptive words to more fully explain how God destroys the weapons we use to fight each other, such as *cuts* and *burns*. The fact that he also "maketh wars to cease unto the ends of the earth" reveals his power over nations. If he can make nations stop fighting each other, how much more can he help individuals end their conflicts with each other?

While God possesses great power to end conflict, your neighbor, professor, counselor, or best friend does not. People can offer techniques, theories, and methods they may claim work for them. But they have no power to resolve disagreements or the ability to influence the human heart to settle disputes as God does.

> The king's heart is in the hand of the Lord, as the rivers of water: he turneth it whithersoever he will. (Proverbs 21:1)

> The heart is deceitful above all things, and desperately wicked: who can know it? I the Lord search the heart, I try the reins, even to give every man according to his ways, and according to the fruit of his doings (Jeremiah 17: 9-10)

An example which demonstrates how God influences our hearts to try to get us to make peace with each other, is an instance where David encountered King Saul in a cave.

> And he came to the sheepcotes by the way, where was a cave; and Saul went in to cover his feet: and David and his men remained in the sides of the cave. And the men of David said unto him, Behold the day of which the Lord said unto thee Behold, I will deliver thine enemy into thine hand, that thou mayest do to him as it shall seem good unto thee. Then David arose and cut the skirt of Saul's robe privily. And it came to pass afterward, that David's heart "smote" him, because he had cut off Saul's skirt. And he said unto his men, The Lord forbid that I should do this thing unto my master, the lord's anointed, to stretch forth mine hand against him, seeing as he is the anointed of the Lord. So David stayed his servants with these words, and suffered them not to rise up against Saul. (1 Samuel 24: 3-7a)

Saul had made David his enemy, and he and his men were chasing David, to try to kill him. When Saul went into the dark cave to relieve himself (go to the bathroom), he had no idea that David and his mighty men were hiding from him there. When David's men realized that King Saul was there and he did not know David was there, they encouraged David to kill him.

But, when David tried to kill Saul, his heart "smote him. This was God dealing with his heart, to convict him (convince him it was wrong to kill Saul). By convicting David this way, God stopped David from killing Saul, which led him to have discussions with Saul to try to resolve their conflict. God moves upon our hearts to try to bring peace the same way he did with David in this situation.

We can trust God to help us settle our differences because he promises to do so, and he keeps his promises. In Proverbs 16:7, God gives us his promise to end our conflicts.

> When a man's ways please the Lord, he makes even his enemies be at peace with him.

According to this passage, God releases his power to make peace when we obey the guidance he gives us in his word (the Scriptures). We can be confident and sure that God will help us because *he keeps his promise to do this when we obey his word.*

The Bible gives us examples of how God ends disputes in the lives of people who obey him. One example is how he settled the dispute between Joseph (the son of Jacob) and his brethren. When Joseph's brothers threw him into a pit and sold him into slavery, resolution of the conflict seemed impossible (see Genesis 37:12–36).

But it wasn't impossible with the help of God. When God began to work in Joseph's life, he made Joseph forget about the pain he suffered in his father's house.

> And Joseph called the name of his firstborn Manasseh: For God, said he, hath made me forget all my toil, and all my father's house. (Genesis 41:51)

The work God did in Joseph's life eventually allowed him to forgive his brothers and reconcile with them.

> And Joseph said unto his brethren, Come near to me, I pray you. And they came near. And he said, I am Joseph your brother, whom ye sold into Egypt. Now therefore, be not grieved nor

angry with yourselves, that ye sold me hither: for God did send me before you to preserve life...And he fell upon his brother Benjamin's neck, and wept; and Benjamin wept upon his neck. Moreover he kissed all his brethren, and wept upon them: and after that his brethren talked with him. (Genesis 45: 4-5, 14-15)

Another example of how God ends disputes is what God did to resolve the disagreement between Esau and Jacob. When Jacob defrauded Esau of his inheritance, Esau was so angry that he planned to kill Jacob.

And Esau hated Jacob because of the blessing wherewith his father blessed him: and Esau said in his heart, The days of mourning for my father are at hand; then I will slay my brother Jacob. (Genesis 27:41)

However, when God changed Esau's heart, Esau loved Jacob passionately, and they reconciled.

And Esau ran to meet him, and embraced him, and fell on his neck, and kissed him: and they wept. (Genesis 33:4)

The fact that Esau wept and ran to hug Jacob shows how deeply God transformed Esau's heart.

A third example of how God ends disputes is what he did to end the conflict between Isaac and the men of Gerar. When these men repeatedly stole the wells that Isaac's men had dug and refused to make peace with Isaac, Isaac dug other wells instead of fighting with them. Although resolution of this conflict looked impossible, God suddenly ended the dispute.

And Isaac's servants digged in the valley, and there found a well of springing water. And the herdmen of Gerar did strive with Isaac's herdmen, saying, The water is ours: and he called the

Preparation for Resolution

> name of the well Esek; because they strove with him. And they digged another well, and they strove for that also: and he called the name Sitnah [hatred]. And he moved from there and dug another well, and they did not quarrel over it. So he called its name Rehoboth, because he said, For now the Lord has made room for us, and we shall be fruitful in the land. (Genesis 26:19–22)

It isn't clear whether God moved these men's hearts or forced them to stop fighting, but because of the stubbornness of the men of Gerar and their resistance to making peace, we know it took a mighty move by God to resolve this issue. Isaac knew God had done this, and this is why he testified that the "Lord has made room for us."

I witnessed God's faithfulness to resolve conflict in my own life when God rebuilt the broken relationship my father and I had with each other. Until I had a particular argument with my father, I didn't realize my father and I talked *at* each other instead of *to* each other. This style of discourse created communication difficulties, misunderstandings, and a great deal of conflict between us. God, however, worked supernaturally to tear down the walls between us when I cared for my father when he became ill with cancer.

One thing God did was deliver my father from the destructive anger he had lived with for years; this occurred during one of our morning Bible studies. That day, for some reason, I felt compelled to read aloud the following passage (1 John 3:11–12).

> For this is the message that ye have heard from the beginning, that we should love one another. Not as Cain, who was of that wicked one, and slew his brother. And wherefore slew he him? Because his own works were evil, and his brother righteous.

This passage deeply touched my father, and he said the following words to me: "Lester, you see that man Cain? I get angry just like he did, and I hurt people with my anger."

His words shocked me. I sensed the Holy Ghost conviction had come upon him and led him to respond this way. I then, gently, said to him, "Daddy, you don't have stay angry this way. God can set you free. Do you want to pray with me and ask God to set you free?"

When my father said yes, I led him in a prayer of deliverance that took away the anger that had plagued him for years and brought peace into his heart.

God ended our conflict, and we built a greater relationship than we'd ever had. Because God did this for my father and me, I trusted God's promises in Malachi 4:6, which states that he "will turn the hearts of the fathers to the children, and the hearts of the children to the fathers." Because God fulfilled his promise in my life, I trust and have confidence in him. *However, I should not place my confidence and trust in my friends, professors, or counselors, because they do not have the same power God possesses.* Because of this, they cannot make and keep the same promises to release me from conflict that God can. Because our friends and neighbors lack the power God has to help us settle our differences, we fail miserably when we place our trust in them rather than in God.

If you've been putting your trust in yourself or other people to settle conflicts, I encourage you to repent and place your trust in the Lord by praying a simple prayer such as this:

> *Father in heaven, I realize that putting my trust in other people— including my friends, professors, or counselors—and their techniques or methods is wrong. Please forgive me and help me put my trust in you. I will obey your word. I ask you to show me your faithfulness by carrying out your promise to help me resolve my conflicts as I walk in ways that please you. I ask you to release your power in my life to do this. In Jesus's name, amen.*

CHAPTER 2

SEEK GOD

I am he which searcheth the reins and hearts: and I will give unto every one of you according to your works.
—REVELATIONS 2:23

And he that searcheth the hearts knoweth what is in the mind of the Spirit, because he maketh intercession for the saints according to the will of God.
—ROMANS 8:27

IN PSALM 139:23–24, David asked God to search his heart.

> Search me, O God, and know my heart: try me and know my thoughts: And see if there be any wicked way in me, and lead me in the way everlasting.

Many of us need to ask God to prepare our hearts to make us ready to engage in meaningful discussions. If we have qualities or behaviors that hinder our ability to discuss and resolve our disagreements, having discussions may be a waste of time. In cases like this, we first should allow God to touch or turn our hearts before we engage in discussions with those with whom we are experiencing conflict.

Jesus addressed this issue when a man asked him to help him resolve a disagreement he had with his brother over an inheritance.

> And one of the company said unto him, Master, speak to my brother, that he may divide the inheritance with me. (Luke 12:13)

Jesus could have spent a few hours meeting with these men and hearing their stories to try to resolve their conflict. But he chose not to do so.

> And he [Jesus] said unto him, Man, who made me a judge or a divider over you? (Luke 12:14)

Instead he gave them a word about the covetousness in their hearts, which was hindering them from resolving their conflict.

> And he said to them, Take heed, and beware of covetousness: for a man's life consisteth not in the abundance of the things which he possesseth. (Luke 12:15)

Why did Jesus do this? The greed of these two men provoked them to be unfair with each other. As long as greed controlled them, discussion would be a waste of time because each one would justify why he was entitled to a larger share than his brother. Instead of wasting time, Jesus decided to first deal with the greed in their hearts. If he could change these men's hearts by getting them to repent for their greed, their selfishness would die. Then they could be fair with each other and resolve the disagreement and perhaps future disagreements.

Jesus used the same approach when his disciples were fighting over which of them was the greatest.

> And he came to Capernaum: and being in the house he asked them, What was it that ye disputed among yourselves by the way? (Mark 9:33)

Instead of Jesus sitting down with them and having a lengthy discussion to hear their stories, he first dealt with the pride and lust (ungodly desires) in their hearts, which lay at the root of the conflict.

> And he sat down, and called the twelve, and saith unto them, If any man desire to be first, the same shall be last of all, and servant of all. (Mark 9:36)

The pride and ungodly desires of these men kept them at odds with one another. If the disciples repented for the issues that hindered resolution, they would be more prepared to sit down and could settle their differences.

Like the feuding brothers as well as Jesus' disciples, most of us have issues in our hearts that we must first deal with to enable us to have meaningful discussions. I want to share some of the issues that you may need to ask God to deal with in you.

You may be suffering from the hurt and unbearable pain of betrayal, disappointment, or abuse.

> Yea, mine own familiar friend, in whom I trusted, which did eat of my bread, hath lifted up his heel against me. (Psalm 41:9)

> For it was not an enemy that reproached me; then I could have borne it: neither was it he that hated me that did magnify himself against me: then I would have hid myself from him: But it was thou, a man mine equal, my guide and mine acquaintance. We took sweet counsel together, and walked into the house of God in company. (Psalm 55:12-14)

Someone I witnessed who suffered such unbearable pain was a little child I represented who was removed from his home because he had contracted from someone there the venereal disease known as Chlamydia. This child was so devastated by the evil done to him that he barely talked. He plummeted into a world where he totally isolated himself, and he allowed very few people in. Someone who has suffered like this is in no condition to confront or have discussions with the person who hurt him.

If this is the case with you, God must heal you to make you emotionally ready for discussion.

> He hath sent me to heal the brokenhearted. (Luke 4:18)

One example in which we see God's ability to heal people to make them emotionally ready to have discussions occurred when he dealt with Isaac regarding his fear.

> And the Lord appeared unto him the same night, and said, I am the God of Abraham thy father; fear not, for I am with thee, and will bless thee, and multiply thy seed for my servant Abraham's sake. (Genesis 26:24)

In this chapter of the Bible, I believe Isaac was afraid of King Abimelech because Abimelech had wrongly expelled him from the land of the Philistines because he was jealous of him (see Genesis 26:12–17). Many of us become fearful or reluctant to talk to the people who deeply hurt us because we do not want to be hurt again.

Right after God delivered Isaac of his fear, God opened the door for him and Abimelech to have discussions to end their disagreement.

> Then Abimelech went to him from Gerar, and Ahuzzah one of his friends, and Phichol the chief captain of his army...And they said, We saw certainly that the Lord was with thee; and we said, Let there be now an oath between us and thee, and let us make covenant with thee. (Genesis 26:26, 28)

You also may need to be delivered from fear (fear of bad results, fear of confrontation, fear of the person with whom you are in conflict) to prepare yourself for having discussions.

In addition you may need to ask God to make you forget the terrible pain you have endured, just as God did for Joseph when his brothers threw him into a pit and sold him into slavery.

> And Joseph called the name of his firstborn Manasseh: For God, said he, hath made me forget all my toil, and all my father's house. (Genesis 41:51)

Deliverance from this pain enabled Joseph to make peace with his brothers.

> And Joseph said unto them, Fear not: for am I in the place of God. But as for you, ye thought evil against me; but God meant it unto good, to bring to pass, as it is this day, to save much people alive. Now therefore fear ye not: I will nourish you, and your little ones. And he comforted them, and spake kindly unto them. (Genesis 50:19–21)

You may be so bitter, angry, hateful, unforgiving, or resentful that you cannot rationally discuss your differences with the person with whom you are in conflict.

> A brother offended is harder to be won than a strong city: and their contentions are like the bars of a castle. (Proverbs 18:19)

If your hearts haven't changed, you and the person you are in conflict with will yell and scream at each other. And things will get worse instead of better. You must ask God to deal with the destructive anger in your hearts that causes you to stir up strife with each other.

> He that is soon angry dealeth foolishly: and a man of wicked devices is hated. (Proverbs 14:17)

> An angry man stirreth up strife, and a furious man aboundeth in transgression. (Proverbs 29:22)

You also must ask God to "turn your heart" to make you forgiving and more receptive to having productive discussions.

> And he shall turn the heart of the fathers to the children, and the heart of the children to the fathers, lest I come and smite the earth with a curse. (Malachi 4:6)

Some of you are so stubborn and inflexible that you are unwilling to see things any way but your way.

> But they and our fathers dealt proudly, and hardened their necks, and hearkened not to thy commandments. And refused to obey, neither were mindful of the wonders thou didst among them. (Nehemiah 9:16–17)

If this is you, ask God to soften your heart so that you become willing to listen to others and accept reasonable compromises to settle your differences.

Some of you have other negative qualities in your hearts—for example pride, jealousy, and ungodly desires—that cause you to stir up strife. These qualities hinder you from having meaningful discussions.

> Hatred stirreth up strifes. (Proverbs 10:12)

> He that is of a proud heart stirreth up strife. (Proverbs 28:25)

> From whence come wars and fightings among you? come they not hence, even of your lusts that war in your members? (James 4:1)

Because of this, you must ask God to unveil these negative qualities to you so that you can repent and be free in order to have fruitful discussions.

Search me, O God, and know my heart: try me and know my thoughts: And see if there be any wicked way in me, and lead me in the way everlasting. (Psalm 139:23–24)

God is willing to touch and transform our hearts to help prepare us for discussion. *But we must be willing to yield to God as he enters our hearts to change us.*

Before you read any further, I encourage you—if you haven't already done so—to go to the altar and ask God to search your heart and cleanse it of any negative qualities.

CHAPTER 3

Pray for God's Will

And he was withdrawn from them about a stone's cast, and kneeled down and prayed, Saying, Father if thou be willing, remove this cup from me: nevertheless, not mine will but thine be done.
—Luke 22:41–42

Jesus instructs us to do the following in Matthew 6:9–10:

> After this manner therefore pray ye: Our Father which art in heaven, Hallowed be thy name. Thy kingdom come, Thy will be done in earth, as it is in heaven.

Jesus not only taught his disciples to pray this way but also taught them to live this way by his example in the garden of Gethsemane.

> And he went forward a little and fell on the ground, and prayed that, if it were possible, the hour might pass from him. And he said, Abba, Father, all things are possible unto thee: take away this cup from me: nevertheless not what I will, but what thou wilt. (Mark 14:35–36)

At times, conflict can be seemingly impossible to handle. You may feel alone, like Jesus did when he prayed in the garden of Gethsemane when Judas betrayed him, and the elders, Pharisees, priests, and scribes planned to have him killed. But no matter how difficult things get, you need to connect with our Father in heaven in prayer, just as Jesus did. I've found this makes all the difference in the world in determining whether you can settle disagreements with others. You also should put your will on the shelf and always pray to God, "Not my will, but thy will be done."

Most of us who are engaged in conflict have an idea of how we want things to go and how we want God to end our conflict. If you ask God to do things your way or to let your will be done, selfishness may be motivating you. If this is the case, ask God to eliminate your selfish desires and to replace them with his will and desires.

Paul encourages us to have the attitude of Christ, in which we think of others (including those we are in conflict with) and not just ourselves.

> Let nothing be done through strife or vainglory; but in lowliness of mind let each esteem other better than themselves. Look not every man on his own things, but every man on the things of others. (Philippians 2:3–4)

Jesus encourages us, as his disciples, to deny ourselves instead of thinking about ourselves first when we try to resolve conflict.

> Then Jesus said unto his disciples, If any man will come after me, let him deny himself, and take up his cross, and follow me. (Matthew 16:24)

When you seek God's will and his kingdom, he will provide the wisdom, power, and everything else you need to settle your differences with another individual.

(For after all these things do the Gentiles seek:) for your heavenly Father knoweth that you need all these things. But seek ye first the kingdom of God, and his righteousness; and all things will be added unto you. (Matthew 6:32–33)

CHAPTER 4

Pray for Each Other

> *Now therefore restore the man his wife: for he is a prophet, and he shall pray for thee, and thou shalt live..So Abraham prayed unto God: and God healed Abimelech, and his wife, and his maidservants, and they bare children.*
> —Genesis 20:7, 17

Jesus says we should take the following step when we are in conflict with each other.

> But I say to you, love your enemies, bless those who curse you, do good to those who hate you, and pray for those who spitefully use you and persecute you, that you may be the sons of your Father in heaven.(Matthew 5:44–45)

Some of us have made the people we are in conflict with our enemies. As children of God, we must reach out to these individuals with love and pray for them. In fact we should start praying for each other as soon as we know or believe we have a misunderstanding or conflict with someone. This is part of our pursuing peace by taking immediate action to try to end our conflict.

> Depart from evil, and do good; seek peace, and pursue it. (Psalm 34:14)

When we pray for the people with whom we are in conflict, we should ask God to heal them, bless them, deliver them, help them, forgive them, and transform them. Some people refuse, however, to pray this way because they are offended.

> A brother offended is harder to be won than a strong city: and their contentions are like the bars of a castle.(Proverbs 18:19)

These people often are very angry with the people who are at odds with them. When this passage says, "and their contentions are like the bars of a castle," it means offended individuals put up walls to separate themselves from others. They also make arguments and excuses as to why they are justified to remain offended.

Some of these people are offended with God. They feel they are right to be angry at God for allowing others to badly hurt them and for not defending them.

Although our flesh may fight against praying for those we are in conflict with, we must take authority over our flesh and take this step in obedience to God. Before we can pray this way, however, most of us must ask God to forgive us for harboring unforgiveness toward him and each other. We also must ask God to grace us with the ability to pray this way, because it is impossible for us to do this without God's help.

As we pray for each other, God often changes our hearts. Sometimes he takes away our stony (i.e., hardened, resistant) hearts and gives us hearts of flesh (Ezekiel 11:19). This helps better prepare us to have meaningful discussions.

According to God's word, God transforms us and heals us when we pray for those with whom we are in conflict. Job experienced this when God told him to pray for his comforters, who argued with him.

> Therefore take unto you now seven bullocks and seven rams, and go to my servant Job, and offer up for yourselves a burnt offering: and my servant Job shall pray for you. And the Lord turned the captivity of Job, when he prayed for his friends:(Job 42:8,10)

As a result, Job was delivered from conflict, and his relationship with his friends was restored.

Abraham and Abimelech also experienced this when they were in conflict with each other. God healed Abimelech and his family when he instructed Abraham to pray for them.

> Now therefore restore the man his wife: for he is a prophet, and he shall pray for thee, and thou shalt live...So Abraham prayed unto God: and God healed Abimelech, and his wife and his maidservants, and they bare children.(Genesis 20:7, 17)

In James 5:16, God confirms that he will heal us and do much more than that when we pray for each other.

> Confess your faults one to another, and pray one for another that you may be healed. The fervent, effectual prayer of the righteous man availeth much.

When people in conflict pray for each other, Jesus makes it clear that he will hear and answer these "prayers of agreement" by helping us settle our disagreements.

> Again I say unto you, That if two of you shall agree on earth as touching anything they shall ask, it shall be done for them of my Father which is in heaven. For where two or three are gathered

together in my name, there am I in the midst of them.(Matthew 18:19–20)

In addition you should pray for the person you are in conflict with regardless of whether he or she prays for you. David did this when the people he was in conflict did evil to him.

> They rewarded me evil for good to the spoiling of my soul. But as for me, when they were sick, my clothing was sackcloth: I humbled myself with fasting; and my prayer returned into mine own bosom. I behaved myself as though he had been my friend or brother: I bowed down heavily, as one that mourneth for his mother. But in mine adversity they rejoiced, and gathered themselves together.(Psalm 35:12–15)

Some people get discouraged and stop praying for the other person when they find out that person refuses to pray for them. But God wants you to pray for that person despite his or her disobedience. God will not allow the other person's failure to obey him to hold you hostage. When you obey God and pray for the other person, God will bless you and set you free.

CHAPTER 5

TACKLE REPEATED CONFLICT

*Then came Peter to him, and said, Lord, how oft shall
my brother sin against me, and I forgive him? Till
seven times? Jesus saith unto him, I say not unto thee,
Until seven times: But until seventy times seven.*
—MATTHEW 18:21–22

BEFORE WE MOVE on to the topic of discussions during conflicts, I want to take a moment to address the subject of repeated conflict with others. I'd like to address this issue because, in my experience, people who are engaged in repeated conflict often feel a great deal of pain, hopelessness, and frustration that they need help and encouragement to overcome.

Some of you may still be feeling hostility, mistrust, and suspicion toward someone, which will make it more difficult for you to resolve your differences through discussion. The malice that people in conflict feel towards each other is sometimes so great that it is very hard to get them to sit down and talk to each other.

I encountered such reluctance to have discussion when I was helping a large family in conflict settle the estate of their deceased mother. Most of the brothers and sisters were so angry at each other that they

Preparation for Resolution

were no longer speaking to each other. But a glimmer of hope came when one of the family members approached me to see if I could facilitate discussion between he and one of his sisters with the hope that they could reconcile. The relative who was approached rejected the overture to make peace because she felt that she had suffered enough heartache over the conflict in her family. She did not want to suffer any more pain and open herself up to more arguments by having further discussions over the same issues. Prior conflict often makes us reluctant to make peace when the door opens up for people to settle their differences.

Peter's words to Jesus in Matthew 18:21 express some of the frustration you may feel when you repeatedly have been conflict with one or more individuals.

You may have started arguing with each other in January, and then you apologized and made peace with each other in February. Then in March you argued over the same thing then sat down and made peace in May. In some cases this pattern of arguing, apologizing, making peace, then arguing again continues with no end in sight.

When Peter says, "How long shall I forgive him?" you probably can feel his frustration. Peter probably was saying to Jesus, "We've gone through the same conflict over and over. He keeps apologizing, but we keep having the same problem. I'm wondering whether his apology is sincere. How long should I put up with this?"

To give you a small taste of what people who have repeated conflicts go through, I'd like to share a story about how I tried to help resolve a conflict a person had with his next-door neighbor. Before this man came to me for counsel and assistance, he and his neighbor had tried many times to talk to each other to settle their differences, but their discussions got them nowhere. As time went on, things got so bad that these men were about to have a physical altercation, and they had to call the police on each other a number of times to keep them from fighting and hurting each other.

By the time this man came to me for help, he was so frustrated with the situation that he had no hope that things would get better or could be resolved by both parties having further discussions or agreeing to go to mediation. Taking his neighbor to court and having a judge hear and decide his case was the only solution he could think of. The following words are a paraphrase of what he said to me when he came to me for help: "This situation is hopeless. We've already tried to discuss things numerous times, but it didn't work. So what good will further discussion or mediation do? He wants to have his way. And as long as he's so stubborn and unwilling to listen or change, there's no hope for settling this. What good will discussion do?"

This man wasn't alone in his feelings. I know other individuals who are now in conflict with others, and they're hesitant or totally unwilling to have discussions with the people they're in conflict with. They repeatedly rehearse in their minds how their past discussions went and how both parties plummeted into a war of words or a full-scale argument. As they do this, they say to themselves, *I've been here before. What's the use in doing this again?*

If you're going through a similar situation, you may have given up hope. But I want to share some words with you to try to give you renewed hope and confidence in God so that you may prepare your heart to have discussions again and allow God to end your conflict.

Seek help from others. When people have had unsuccessful discussions, I usually encourage them to seek out mediation help (in which a mediator or peacemaker helps facilitate discussion). This is what Jesus tells us to do: "But if he will not hear thee, then take one or two more, that in the mouth of two or three witnesses every word may be established"(Matthew 18:16).

Although you've had discussions with the other party, these discussions probably weren't effective. In many cases people in conflict do more yelling and screaming at each other than sharing their hearts and hearing each other. In cases like this, you should seek out a skillful mediator who isn't emotionally involved in the conflict. A mediator such as this can help calm down you and the other person and help you leave behind your malice and hostility toward each other so you can engage in meaningful discussion. The Bible confirms that a good peacemaker can do this: "He that is slow to anger appeases strife" (Proverbs 15:18).

Stop looking at the past and blaming the other person. You may be right when you say the other person is stubborn and unwilling to listen or change. But as long as you continue to look at past failures and play the blame game, you'll likely be reluctant to move forward and get the resolution assistance you need to help bring your conflict to an end. In Philippians 3:15 Paul encourages us to leave the past behind when he says, "But this one thing that I do, forgetting those things which are behind, and reaching forth unto the things which are before, I press toward the mark for the prize of the high calling of God in Christ Jesus."

Trust God to help you. Although you may be frustrated and feel as if you have no hope, God can provide hope in hopeless situations. Earlier in the book, I briefly described how God moved to resolve the conflict between Esau and Jacob. Who could have imagined that Esau would ever stop hating Jacob? But it happened. God moved his heart so mightily that he ran to meet Jacob, and they wept when they finally came face-to-face (see Genesis 33:4). Our God is awesome to have done such an impossible thing.

Earlier in the book (in the chapter titled, "Trusting God"), I shared how God moved mightily to deliver my father from anger and reconcile us. I have witnessed God do this and other mighty things in my relationships. So I encourage you to turn your heart to him and trust him.

Although you may have failed to resolve your differences with a person in prior discussions, God can turn things around and transform your failure into success if you put your trust in him. The story of Peter catching the fish in chapter five of the Book of Luke demonstrates this truth about God.

Peter was just like you. He fished all night but caught nothing. Because of his failure, his situation looked hopeless. But things quickly turned around when Peter let down his net, as Jesus advised him to do. Peter caught so many fish that his nets broke, and he had to get the help of other fishermen to bring in the great multitude of fish he caught that day.

And when they had this done, they enclosed a great multitude of fishes; and the net broke. And they beckoned unto their partners, which were in the other ship, that they should come and help them. And they came, and filled the ship, so that they began to sink.(Luke 5:6–7)

Let's make Peter's story practical to you and your situation. Even though your efforts at discussion may have failed, just like Peter's initial effort to catch fish, your next attempt at discussion or mediation can be as successful as Peter's attempt at fishing if you place the situation in God's hands instead of handling the discussion yourself.

God knows your hearts, and he's able to make things work in your life in ways that you cannot. So trust him, and ask him to help you have a discussion with the other person again: "If any of you lack wisdom, let him ask of God, that gives to all men liberally, and upbraids not; and it shall be given him."(James 1: 4)

On a final note, if you repeatedly are engaged in conflict with the same person, seek guidance from God regarding what is at the root of the conflict that produces this cycle. Instead of blaming the other person, pray for the individual and yourself so God can reveal and address with you the root cause of the problem and you both can be set free. If God reveals to you any role or part that you have played that has started or contributed to the conflict, repent and ask him to forgive you and change you.

CHAPTER 6

ENGAGE IN DISCUSSION

Therefore if you bring your gift to the altar, and there remember your brother has something against you, leave your gift before the altar and go your way. First be reconciled to your brother, and then come and offer your gift.
—MATTHEW 5:23–24

JESUS INSTRUCTS US to do the following:

> Moreover if your brother sins against you, go and tell him his fault between you and him alone. If he hears you, you have gained your brother.(Matthew 18:15)

We should have discussions to settle any misunderstandings or differences we have with each other. We also should have discussions as part of pursuing peace with each other.

> Let him eschew evil, and do good; let him seek peace, and ensue it.(1 Peter 3:11)

Preparation for Resolution

While we pursue peace, our goal should be to initiate discussion and seek peace with the person we are in conflict with as soon as possible. When Jesus was in conflict with others, he often immediately took steps to initiate discussions with them.

> And immediately when Jesus perceived in his spirit that they so reasoned within themselves, he said unto them, Why reason ye these things in your hearts? (Mark 2:8)

If you don't arrange to have discussions immediately because you feel you aren't ready to talk with the other person, immediately go to the altar and ask God to prepare you to engage in discussion as soon as possible.

When you discuss your differences with an individual in a way that pleases God, God shows up and will help you end your disagreement.

> For where two or three are gathered together in my name there am I in the midst of them.(Matthew 18:20)

God brings in an atmosphere of peace, and he deals with your heart. What I experienced in a mediation session with a couple who was going through marital difficulties provides an example of what God will do in these situations. When the couple started one of the sessions, they were very angry with each other. They refused to look at each other, and they spoke only to me. But in the middle of the session, a shift occurred. They both calmed down, and their facial expressions began to change. Their words went from being harsh to gentle. And instead of looking at me, they began to look at each other and talk to each other. This couple proceeded to talk to each other this way for about fifteen minutes as I sat and listened to their meaningful dialogue. After I explained this shift and how they now were speaking to each other, they were amazed that they were talking to each other this way.

This shift was a move of God that God brought about to help the people in conflict hear each other and end their differences. When you allow God's presence to come in as it did on this day, you'll see this kind of shift occur during your discussions.

God also gives you words to say and wisdom to end your differences, which occurred in the encounter between David and Amasai. When David and his men were fighting to gain control of Israel, David was approached by a group of men he wasn't sure he could trust.

> And there came of the children of Benjamin and Judah to the hold unto David.(1 Chronicles 12:16)

David initiated discussions with them to find out what their intentions were.

> And David went out to meet them, and answered and said to them, If ye be come peaceably unto me to help me, mine heart shall be knit unto you: but if ye be come to betray me to mine enemies, seeing there is no wrong in mine hands, the God of our fathers look thereon, and rebuke it.(1 Chronicles 12:17)

When David did this, the Holy Spirit moved upon Amasai and gave him words of peace to speak to David.

> Then the spirit came upon Amasai, who was the chief of the captains, and he said, Thine are we, David, and on thy side, thou son of Jesse: peace, peace be unto thee, and peace be to thine helpers: for thy God helpeth thee. (1 Chronicles 12:18)

As Amasai spoke these Holy Spirit–generated words, the Spirit touched David's heart, causing him to make peace with these men.

> Then David received them, and made them captains of the band. (1 Chronicle 12:18)

Preparation for Resolution

Just as God moved the hearts of these men to make peace with one another, God longs to move the hearts of people in conflict to have meaningful discussions. We must be prepared to yield to God to allow this and other beneficial things to happen when we come together for discussion. In the chapters that follow, we'll look closely at important aspects of discussion so that we'll be better prepared for it.

Chapter 7

Identify Major and Minor Issues

> *I therefore, the prisoner of the Lord, beseech you that ye walk worthy of the vocation wherewith ye are called, with all lowliness and meekness, with longsuffering, forbearing one another with love; Endeavoring to keep the unity of the Spirit in the bond of peace.*
> —Ephesians 4:1–3

Before you try to have a discussion to resolve a conflict, determine whether what you're upset about is a major or minor issue, because this will determine how you should deal with the situation and the conflict. Minor issues are concerns or objections you have about a person or his or her behavior that are inconsequential and that you should overlook and not discuss.

> The discretion of a man is to deferreth his anger; and it is a glory to pass over a transgression.(Proverbs 19:11)

Here are some examples of minor issues. You're upset with Sally because she doesn't carry out the ministry of service (or helps) in the church the same way that you would if you were doing it. As long as Sally has performed well and has done nothing wrong, you shouldn't make her differences with you or the way she does things a point of contention. God has uniquely made all of us, and he uses our gifts in different ways. This means that we should learn how to understand our differences and be more tolerant of each other instead of thinking that "our way is the right way" and "their way is the wrong way."

You're upset with Bob because he came late to an important rehearsal. This is the only time he's ever been late. He had an emergency and had to take his daughter to the hospital. You should overlook his tardiness in this instance. His daughter's life and health are much more important than a rehearsal.

Overlooking our brother's fault is called forbearance. God encourages us to walk in forbearance toward each other, because none of us is perfect. We all have faults that we should overlook in each other.

> Put on therefore, as the elect of God, holy and beloved, bowels of mercies, kindness, humbleness of mind, meekness, longsuffering; Forbearing one another, and forgiving one another, if any man have a quarrel against any. (Colossians 3:12-13)

Major faults are serious things we do to each other (such as lie, cheat, steal, defraud, abuse, or betray) that we should not overlook. When people do things such as this, we must talk with them to ensure they make necessary changes in their behavior. We must do this to end our conflict and improve our relationship with them. In this vein Matthew 18:15 states, "Go and tell him his fault, between you and he alone."

When we overlook the major faults of others and refuse to address these issues with them, they will do the same terrible things to us over and over. And we will suffer as a result. So we must speak the truth to each other in love in order to address and resolve these issues.

If we treat a person's minor faults as if they are major, the person may get angry at us for being too critical or judgmental. In the United States, we have slang expressions we use when people do this—these individuals are "nitpicking" or "making a mountain out of a molehill." When this occurs, the conflict will get worse instead of better.

CHAPTER 8

Speak in Gentle Tones

*A soft answer turns away wrath;
but grievous words stir up anger.*
—Proverbs 15:1

We should prepare ourselves to speak in gentle, respectful tones instead of yelling and screaming in anger. When we yell, our discussion accomplishes nothing. However, when we gently speak to each other, we can resolve our differences.

We can be gentle, however, only if we have allowed God to deliver us from any tendencies toward anger we may have. If you haven't already asked God to unveil any destructive anger that's hindering your ability to discuss and resolve your differences, here are a few questions to ask yourself to see whether you have an anger problem.

Lingering Anger
Have you remained angry with the person you are in conflict with for more than twenty-four hours? Ephesians 4:26–27 makes it clear that harboring anger for more than a day is a problem: "Let not the sun go

down on your wrath: neither give place to the devil." Even if you feel justified in your anger, God wants it to last no more than a day.

This reminds me of a mediation I handled in which a woman accused her employer of discrimination. As soon as the mediation started, the woman attacked her boss with repeated angry outbursts. Although I counseled her to calm down and warned her that further outbursts would cause the mediation to end, she couldn't do as I asked. After five outbursts on her part in twenty minutes, the employer's representatives left the table and ended the settlement conference.

This was one of the worst cases I'd ever seen of a person losing control because she harbored so much anger and resentment. What made this situation so sad is that the woman had come so far to have this discussion but got nothing done. She had traveled about two hundred miles to Baltimore only to leave after being there for thirty minutes. What a waste of time. This incident shows us the terrible impact anger can have on our ability to have meaningful discussions.

Rage and Fury
Does the mention of the name of the person you're in conflict with or what they did make you incensed or tick you off?

I witnessed this kind of anger and what it does when I spoke to a young woman who had a conflict with her father. The two had not spoken to each other in a few years. When our discussion began, she was very calm. However, as she continued to talk about her dad, she became increasingly angry. She then expressed how she hated him and she never wanted to see him again. People with this much anger aren't ready to sit at the settlement table with the person they're at odds with.

In mediations in which one person accuses another of betrayal or adultery, I've seen people manifest rage or boiling anger as soon as the powder-keg issue is raised. This level of anger keeps individuals from being ready to calmly come to the settlement table.

I saw this happen when I was facilitating discussion between two people who had gotten divorced from each other, and they needed to change the child support and child custody arrangements because circumstances in their lives had changed. The two people quietly worked together during the first part of their mediation session. But, when the issue came up that they had split up because one of them had committed adultery, this caused the woman to explode in anger. She lost control, and she called her ex-husband terrible names. She then began to loudly point out the terrible and deceitful behavior that she claims that he did to drive them apart. This woman was so angry about this that she could not go on with the session until I caucused (took her to a private room to have discussion) with her to get her to calm down.

Speed to Anger
Do you get angry quickly, lose control of yourself, and do foolish things? Proverbs 14:17 reveals that this is what people who get angry quickly do: "He that is soon angry doeth foolishly."

People who get angry quickly often have control issues. When things do not go as they want them to, they yell and scream at the person they are upset with. Because of this, these people have a difficult time using discussion to settle their differences.

I witnessed how volatile people can be who get angry quickly when I allowed the family members of a good friend of mine to use my conference room to have discussions with each other. My friend asked me to do this so that his relatives could have a safe and neutral place that they could come to try to settle their differences.

When the family members came to my office, they all appeared to be very friendly. But this changed quickly. A few minutes after they went into my conference room to talk privately, they started shouting and yelling at each other. They became so loud that I and the people in the suites all the way down the hall could hear their conversation. They yelled at each other like this for about ten minutes, and they all left my conference room very angry at each other. People who get angry quickly and lose control as these people did in this situation will not be able to privately discuss and resolve their differences. They will need the help of a mediator who can keep them calm enough to rationally discuss and resolve their differences with each other.

Preparation For Resolution

If you answered yes to any of these questions, or you're harboring the kind of anger exhibited in the examples I mentioned, you should admit that you have a problem with anger and ask God to deliver you from your anger.

When we talk to each other with meekness and gentleness, we often can have productive dialogue. Our gentle words can set an atmosphere of peace. Sometimes they even can dispel the anger in the other person, which makes it easier to talk and make peace with each other. When we use harsh words, the person may become angry or hurt, and the conflict can worsen.

> A soft answer turns away wrath; but grievous words stir up anger.(Proverbs 15:1)

Sometimes our discussion involves correcting each other with meek words instead of harsh language.

> Brethren, if a man be overtaken in a fault, ye which are spiritual, restore such a one in the spirit of meekness; considering thyself, lest thou also be tempted.(Galatians 6:1)

Paul encouraged Timothy to use gentle words whenever conflict arose between him and the members of his congregation.

> And the servant of the Lord must not strive; but be gentle unto all men, apt to teach, patient, in meekness instructing those that oppose themselves; of God peradventure will give them repentance to the acknowledging of the truth; And that they may recover themselves out of the snare of the devil who are taken captive by him at his will.(2 Timothy 2:24–26)

Paul makes it clear that our gentle words have great power. When we speak gentle words, God often moves people's hearts to calm them down. These words may help us end our conflict and deliver our brother or sister out of the snare Satan has set for them.

Speak in Gentle Tones

I experienced the power and calming effect of using gentle words when I worked as an attorney for a child who had been taken from her mother's home by Child Protective Services. Because the mother and the CPS worker had been involved in many heated exchanges, the mother was angry and unwilling to talk to the CPS worker when we were in court for a negotiation session. When I learned that they weren't talking to each other and that this was ruining a possibly good and amicable settlement of the case, I asked the CPS worker, "Do you mind if I try to talk to this mother?" She said, "Go ahead. Give it a try. But it won't do any good."

When I spoke encouraging, reaffirming, gentle words to the mother, her whole attitude changed. Her anger disappeared, and she had a good conversation with the CPS worker that allowed us to amicably settle the case. When the shocked CPS worker asked me what I'd done, I testified to her about the power of God's word to calm people down and change circumstances.

The conflict between Gideon and the men of Ephraim further demonstrates how gentle words can calm people and end conflict. When the men of Ephraim attacked Gideon with accusations, Gideon's gentle words calmed these angry men, and they made peace with each other.

> Now the men of Ephraim said to him, Why have you done this to us by not calling us when you went to fight with the Midianites? And they did chide with him sharply. So he said to them, What have I done in comparison with you? Is not the gleaning of grapes of Ephraim better than the vintage of Abiezer? God has delivered into your hands the princes of Midian, Oreb, and Zeeb. And what was I able to do in comparison with you? Then their anger was abated toward him, when he said that.(Judges 8:1–3)

In the parable of the prodigal son, the father used gentle words to woo his older son to make peace with himself and his other son. The son was angry and bitter because the father gave the younger son a party despite the terrible things the younger son had done.

> And he was angry, and would not go in: therefore came his father out, and entreated him. And he answering said to his father, Lo, these many years do I serve thee, neither transgressed I at any time they commandment; and yet thou never gavest me a kid, that I might make merry with my friends; But as soon as this thy son was come, which hath devoured thy living with harlots, thou hast killed for him the fatted calf. And he said unto him, Son, thou art ever with me, and all that I have is thine. It was meet that we should make merry, and be glad: for this thy brother was dead, and is alive again; and was lost, and is found. (Luke 15:28–32)

When this passage states that the father went out and "entreated" his older son, it means he tried to gently persuade him to stop being bitter and join the festivities and make peace with his younger brother. Our gentle words also can woo people in conflict with us to try to make peace.

When Solomon's son Rehoboam was in conflict with the people of Israel, the elders under Solomon advised him to speak gentle words and they would be at peace with him.

> And the king Rehoboam consulted with the old men, that stood before Solomon his father while he yet lived, and said, How do ye advise that I may answer this people? And they spake unto him, saying, If thou wilt be a servant unto this people this day, and wilt serve them, and answer them, and speak good words to them, then they will be thy servants forever. (1 Kings 12: 6-7)

The different examples we mentioned in this chapter show us that speaking gentle words works. Remaining calm and using gentle words also increases the chances that you can make peace with those with whom you are in conflict.

CHAPTER 9

HAVE THE RIGHT FACTS

And the princes of the children of Ammon said unto Hanun their lord, Thinkest thou that David doth honour thy father, that he hath sent comforters unto thee? Hath not David rather sent his servants to search the city, and to spy it out, and to overthrow it?
—2 SAMUEL 10:3

BEFORE YOU MEET for discussion, do a full investigation to confirm the truth before you accuse anyone of wrongdoing. If you don't do this, and you falsely accuse someone of wrongdoing, you more than likely will make the person angry because no one likes to be falsely accused.

The individual may launch a counterattack against you, and you may end up in all-out warfare. I want to share with you three examples in the Bible in which major conflict broke out when false accusations were made against a person.

One situation involves Ishbosheth accusing Abner of being disloyal to his father King Saul by sleeping with Saul's girlfriend.

Preparation for Resolution

> And Saul had a concubine, whose name was Rizpah, the daughter of Aiah: and Ishbosheth said to Abner, Wherefore hast thou gone into my father's concubine? (2 Samuel 3:7)

In this case we have no idea whether Ishbosheth conducted an investigation to see whether this was true before he accused Abner.

When Abner heard this accusation, he denied it and became very upset. He was so angry with Ishbosheth that he permanently broke off their relationship and made friends with David, Ishbosheth's enemy.

> Then Abner was very wroth for the words of Ishbosheth, and said, Am I a dog's head, which against Judah do show kindness this day to the house of Saul thy father, to his brethren, and to his friends, and have not delivered thee into the hand of David, that thou chargest me today with a fault concerning this woman? So do God to Abner, and more also, except, as the Lord hath sworn to David, even so I do to him; To translate the kingdom from the house of Saul, and set up the throne if David over Israel. (2 Samuel 3:8-10)

This story shows how terrible and destructive conflict can become when we do not have the right facts.

Another incident that confirms how conflict can arise when we make false accusations is the story of King David and the children of Ammon (see 2 Samuel 10:1-19).

When the king of Ammon died, David sent comforters to the king's son, the prince, to show him he supported him. The prince's counselors didn't believe David was sincere, and they thought he was using this act as a ploy to attack and destroy Ammon.

> And the princes of the children of Ammon said unto Hanun their lord, Thinkest thou that David doth honour thy father, that he hath sent comforters unto thee? Hath not David rather sent his servants to search the city, and to spy it out, and to overthrow it? (2 Samuel 10:3)

Instead of contacting David to ask him his motive, the prince believed the word of his servants, who stated that David was out to destroy him, and then he launched an attack against David's men.

David responded to their attack; a war broke out, and many people were killed. This conflict and bloodshed could have been avoided if the children of Ammon had asked David his motive instead of assuming he had evil intentions.

A third incident that reveals that terrible conflict can arise when we make possibly false accusations is the dispute between the twelve tribes of Israel over the altar that two and a half tribes built (see Joshua 22:10–34).

The nine and a half tribes were upset when they heard that the two and a half tribes had built an altar, as they immediately thought it was a forbidden altar to worship idols. Instead of discussing the situation with the two and a half tribes, the armies of the nine and a half tribes gathered and planned to declare war and attack the two and a half tribes.

Thank God someone with wisdom from the nine and a half tribes sent messengers to have discussions with the two and a half tribes to find out what their motive had been in building the altar. When they discussed the situation, the nine and a half tribes learned they were wrong about the intent of the two and a half tribes. They hadn't built a forbidden altar to idols. They had built an altar of remembrance to declare unity between the nine and a half tribes and the two and a half tribes, who now lived on different sides of the Jordan.

When the truth was revealed, warfare was averted, and the two sides made peace. This story reveals how terrible conflict can arise when we make false accusations without conducting an investigation to gather all the facts in a situation.

In many instances I've seen conflict escalate in churches and families when people accuse others without doing an investigation.

If you think a person has done wrong to you, but you aren't sure, gently ask the person a question that will allow you to find out the truth regarding his or her motives. When we make gentle inquiries, people usually will not get angry at us, as they commonly do when we directly and mistakenly attack them for doing something wrong.

King David used this approach when he wasn't certain whether a group of men who came to see him were his enemies or friends.

> And David went out to meet them, and answered and said to them, If ye be come peaceably unto me to help me, mine heart shall be knit unto you: but if ye be come to betray me to mine enemies, seeing there is no wrong in mine hands, the God of our fathers look thereon, and rebuke it.(1 Chronicles 12:17)

When David used the word *if*, he was making it clear that he wasn't accusing these men of doing anything wrong. He merely wanted to find out the truth about them because he wasn't sure of their intentions. When we approach people as David did in this instance, people will be less likely to get upset with us than they would if we used direct, accusatory words against them.

CHAPTER 10

HEAR EACH OTHER

*Wherefore, my beloved brethren, let every man be swift
to hear, slow to speak, slow to wrath: For the wrath
of man worketh not the righteousness of God.*
—JAMES 1:19–20

WE MUST HEAR each other because Jesus reveals that this is a very important step in making peace with each other.

> Moreover if your brother sins against you, go and tell him his fault between you and him alone. If he hears you, you have gained your brother. (Matthew 18:15)

When your brother hears you, you have gained your brother—in other words, reconciled with him.

According to *Strong's Concordance*, the Greek word for "hear" is *akouo* (pronounced "ak-oo-o"). It means to hear, give audience, be reported, or understand. I want to use these definitions to give you a sense of what it means to "hear each other" in real-life conversations.

Preparation for Resolution

When we hear each other, we have a dialogue instead of a one-sided conversation. We take turns speaking to each other. We also listen to each other instead of trying to dominate or control the conversation.

> Wherefore, my beloved brethren, let every man be swift to hear, slow to speak, slow to wrath: For the wrath of man worketh not the righteousness of God.(James 1:19-20)

In cases in which you have tried to dominate or control the entire conversation, it is likely that you did not settle your disagreement because doing this makes the person in conflict with you angry. As long people feel like you are not giving them the chance to share what is on their heart, they will be unwilling to talk with you or settle the dispute. You may need to go back to the person you are in conflict with and apologize for doing this. Your apology may open the door for you to restart the conversation, which may resolve the dispute.

When we hear each other, we communicate by talking *to* each other, rather than *at* each other. God sometimes gives us words to say when we want to communicate effectively with each other. This is exactly what he did to help Amasai have meaningful discussions with David.

> Then the spirit came upon Amasai who was the chief of the captains, and he said, Thine are we, David, and on thy side, thou son of Jesse: peace, peace be unto thee, and peace be to thine helpers: for thy God helpeth thee. (1 Chronicles 12:18)

The fact that the "spirit came upon Amasai" shows that the Holy Ghost gave him the aforementioned words to help him make peace with David.

As we take turns talking, we share with each other what's important to us, such as how we feel and think, why we're upset, and exactly what we want our discussion to accomplish.

In some cases we point out the other person's faults—especially if we feel the person has done something wrong to us—to try to get the person to correct his or her behavior.

As the other person shares, we take the time to listen and to get an understanding of the situation from his or her perspective. When we communicate effectively with each other, we can then have discussions in which we try to arrive at a meeting of the minds to see which issues we can settle. In some cases this ends the conflict and allows us to restore the relationship.

When we truly hear the other person's perspective, it sometimes lets us see that our behavior towards them was improper. We may be blind to this truth and need to have this pointed out to us. so that we can apologize

Also, it sometimes changes the way we feel about the person we're in conflict with. Many times this paves the way for us to make peace with each other.

My wife and I experienced this when we had a misunderstanding with another couple over an issue. This issue had so upset my wife that she lost sleep thinking about it. When she and I considered the matter from our perspective, we thought the issue would lead to a major argument when we discussed it with the other couple. But we were wrong.

When we sat down with the couple, they shared what was in their hearts. About two minutes into the conversation, things immediately changed for my wife and me when we heard they had undertaken the actions they did to try to help us, not hurt us. Once they said this, we realized we had misunderstood their motives. As soon as we heard the truth, we quickly resolved the misunderstanding. What we thought would lead into a quarrel and a war of words turned into a delightful two-hour conversation.

Abraham and Abimelech also experienced this when they had discussions when they were in conflict. Abraham and Sarah were husband and wife. When Abraham told Abimelech that Sarah was his sister, Abimelech believed that Sarah was an unmarried woman, and he wanted to take Sarah as his wife. When Abimelech found out that Abraham had deceived him and Sarah was actually Abraham's wife, Abimelech confronted Abraham about misleading him.

> Then Abimelech called Abraham, and said unto him, What hast thou done unto us? And what have I offended thee, that thou

Preparation For Resolution

> brought on me and on my kingdom a great sin? Thou hast done deeds unto me that thou ought not be done. And Abimelech said unto Abraham, What sawest thou, that thou hast done this thing? (Genesis 20:9-10)

Abimelech was definitely angry with Abraham. You can tell from his words that he was yelling at Abraham. But when he heard things from Abraham's perspective, his feelings about Abraham changed.

> And Abraham said, Because I thought surely the fear of God is not in this place; and they will slay me for my wife's sake. And yet indeed she is my sister, she is the daughter of my father, but not the daughter of my mother; and she became my wife. And it came to pass, when God caused me to wander from my father's house, that I said to her, This is the kindness which thou shalt show unto me; at every place wither we shall come, say of me, He is my brother.(Genesis 20:11-13)

When Abimelech learned that Abraham did not intend to hurt him—rather his actions were motivated by his fear of Abimelech—the king's anger dissipated, and he and Abraham made peace with each other.

> And Abimelech took sheep and oxen, and menservants, and womenservants, and gave them unto Abraham, and restored him Sarah his wife. And Abimelech said, Behold my land is before thee: dwell where it pleaseth thee. So Abraham prayed unto God: and God healed Abimelech and his wife, and his maidservants; and they bare children.(Genesis 20: 14-15, 17)

This is why it is so important that we allow each other to speak and that we carefully listen to what is being said. I'm not saying that hearing each other—as my wife and I did—will always quickly end conflict. Some disagreements and misunderstandings take much more work to resolve. But even with the most complicated conflicts, it may be helpful if you and the person you are at odds with start the conversation by taking a few minutes to share what's in your hearts and let each other know that your motives are good and that you are not out to hurt each other. In some cases doing this can break the ice and erase some of the coldness and anger that exists between you. If you can get this to happen, the door may open for you to move forward so that you may begin to tackle the more difficult issues that are causing conflict in your relationship.

CHAPTER 11

CONFESS YOUR FAULTS

Confess your faults one to another, and pray for one another, that ye may be healed
—JAMES 5: 16

WE CONFESS OUR faults by admitting any part we played in doing something that hurt the other person in the conflict or contributing to starting the conflict. We should do this instead of trying to evade responsibility. One of the reasons why God wants us to confess our faults is because doing this may lead us to forgive each other.

Some people claim you never should admit wrongdoing because people will take advantage of you. I disagree with this because God helps us when we confess our faults to each other.

> He that covereth his sins shall not prosper: but whoso confesseth and forsaketh them shall have mercy. (Proverbs 28:13)

As this passage indicates, God extends his mercy to us when we admit our faults, which helps us settle our differences with each other.

Preparation for Resolution

This is what happened to the apostles when the Christians from Grecia accused them of neglecting the Grecian widows of their daily ministration (see Acts 6:1-7). Instead of trying to evade responsibility or justify their conduct, the apostles admitted their fault. When they did this, God gave them a solution to resolve the issue. And the conflict quickly ended instead of turning into a major division or fight that would split the church.

When my wife and I have conflict with each other, we have found that our disagreements end sooner when we openly and honestly confess our faults to each other. When we do this, we aren't just saying to each other, "I apologize" to try to quickly end the argument. This tactic doesn't work and often makes the other person angrier with you. Rather, my wife and I point out to each other real faults for which we want to be forgiven.

Another real life example that I am familiar with confirms that conflict and the turmoil it brings into our lives can end quickly when we admit our faults. This story involves a congregation member who left our church when one of her friends became offended and left the congregation. When her friend left, the friend and his family quickly settled into a new church home. But, the congregation member never found a suitable congregation and she wandered aimlessly in the wilderness, going from church to church.

About two years after this member left, she returned to visit our congregation. She admitted to me that leaving was wrong, and that she was very sorry that she left. I advised her that, if she wanted to come back, all that she needed to do was to apologize to the Senior Pastor and we would welcome her back.

This former member told me that she was not sure she would come back because she was so ashamed about what she had done, and she thought that the congregation was unwilling to accept her back.

Although I tried to lovingly persuade her to come back, she never did. In her situation, what I said to her was true. All that she had to do was confess her fault, and she would have received a ring and robe just as the Prodigal Son did when he returned to his Father's home (See Luke 15: 21-24). Her turmoil and heartache could have ended quickly.

But she let her pride, fear, guilt and shame stop her from confessing her faults and making peace. Instead of being in a church home where the people loved her, she continued to go from church to church for the next few years.

God also heals our hearts and our relationships when we confess our faults.

> Confess your faults one to another, and pray for one another, that ye may be healed. (James 5:16)

Such a confession allows God to deliver us from the things in our lives that cause us to start conflict and hinder our relationships. God frees us of these things when we confess them to him and to each other.

Confessing our faults may also make a major difference in our lives. Think about what may have happened in Jacob's family if he had done this. Jacob was guilty of favoring Joseph over his other sons, which alienated his children from one another.

> Now Israel loved Joseph more than all of his children, because he was the son of his old age: and he made him a coat of many colors. And when his brethren saw that their father loved him more than all his brethren, they hated him, and could not speak peaceably to him. (Genesis 37:3–4)

If Jacob had apologized to his sons for his wrongdoing, their anger may have dissipated. This, in turn, may have spurred them to make peace with Jacob and Joseph instead of throwing Joseph into a pit and selling him into slavery (see Genesis 37: 23-28). A father's apology to his sons may be pivotal in causing the father's heart to turn to his children and the children's hearts to turn to their father (see Malachi 4:6). As you can see, an apology can have a great impact on families and relationships.

On the other hand, we do not prosper (or have our conflicts resolved) when we cover our sin or evade responsibility. Sometimes an apology breaks the ice and gets us talking to each other. But when we deny any wrongdoing or try to evade responsibility, the other person may remain cold and unresponsive. And then we remain in conflict.

I witnessed the truth of this when two of my dear friends were in marital conflict with each other. The husband was a man I came to know and love over the years. I used to go with him to the services he held at the two nursing homes he ministered at. I stood with him as the best man at his wedding. His wife quickly became a good friend of mine.

The couple had been married for only a year when major rifts broke out between them. One day the husband told me that he had enough, and they planned to get a divorce.

This saddened me. When I shared the bad news with another couple who also loved them, we agreed to try to help them save their marriage. When we asked this couple if they would be willing to sit down with us and have "facilitated discussion," they agreed to do so.

However, on the day we were supposed to meet with the couple, they cancelled the meeting. They smiled at us as if everything was all right. They also told us that they had discussed things and that they had made up with each other.

This couple had lied to us. They had talked, but they settled nothing. Shortly after cancelling the meeting, they filed divorce papers and ended the marriage.

To this day, I have no idea why they refused to meet with us. They may have had feelings of guilt and shame, or they may have thought we would lose respect for them if we learned about the foolish, childish, and selfish things they were doing to each other.

Whatever the reason was, their deception kept the truth from coming out. I believe that this marriage could have been saved if our friends had allowed the meeting to take place and they had been open and honest with us and each other. What makes this story so sad is that this couple was in their seventies when they were fighting and splitting up. When people get as old as my dear friends were, they usually want to live out the rest of their days in peace instead of being in warfare and turmoil. Unfortunately, this did not happen with them.

I also disagree with the argument that people will take advantage of us if we admit our faults. Because God gives us his grace, he will not allow the people we are in conflict with to take advantage of us; in fact the opposite is true. When we do what God says, God will move the hearts of people who oppose us to get them to make peace with us.

> When a man's ways please the Lord, he makes even his enemies to be at peace with him.(Proverbs 16:7)

When we confess our faults in obedience to God, we receive the grace we need to set us free and end our differences with each other.

CHAPTER 12

END CONFLICT

He maketh wars to cease unto the ends of the earth.
—Psalm 46:9

When you engage in discussions with people you have disagreements with, your goal should be to *end* the conflict. This requires that you bring up for discussion and resolution *all the important issues that are causing strife between you*. To do this effectively, you must take the time to identify these issues before you engage in discussion. You also may need to get counsel from a friend who can objectively point out to you a list of important things you should discuss to fully resolve all your issues.

You also should have a full discussion of these issues, one in which you fully air and resolve your differences as Abraham and Abimelech did in Genesis 20. As mentioned, Abimelech was upset with Abraham because Abraham had misled him by not telling him that Sarah was his wife.

> Then Abimelech called Abraham, and said unto him, What hast thou done unto us? And what have I offended thee, that thou

> brought on me and on my kingdom a great sin? Thou hast done deeds unto me that thou ought not be done. And Abimelech said unto Abraham, What sawest thou, that thou hast done this thing? And Abimelech said, Behold my land is before thee; dwell where it pleaseth thee....So Abraham prayed unto God: and God healed Abimelech, and his wife, and his maidservants; and they bare children.(Genesis 20:9-10, 15, 17)

Their initial discussion did not resolve everything. A little while later, Abimelech approached Abraham, and they addressed and resolved the issues that remained between them.

> And it came to pass at the time that Abimelech and Phicol the chief captain of his host, spake unto Abraham, saying, God is with thee in all that thou doest. Now therefore swear unto me here by God that thou wilt not deal falsely with me, nor with my son, nor with my son's son: but according to the kindness that I have done unto thee, thou shalt do unto me, and to the land wherein thou hast sojourned. And Abraham said, I will swear. And Abraham reproved Abimelech because of a well of water, which Abimelech's servants had violently taken away. And Abimelech said, I wot not who hath done this thing: neither didst thou tell me, neither yet heard I of it, but today. And Abraham took sheep and oxen, and gave them unto Abimelech; and both of them made a covenant. (Genesis 21:22-27)

We can glean several important points from this passage. Notice that both men approached each other to address and resolve major issues or faults, which ultimately helped improve their relationship. Abimelech confronted Abraham about false dealing (deceitfulness), and Abraham confronted Abimelech about his men stealing Abraham's wells.

We also see that these men openly and honestly dealt with each other. When Abimelech confronted Abraham, Abraham admitted his fault instead of denying or trying to hide what he had done. Abimelech did the same when Abraham pointed out his fault. Having a full exchange and being open to admitting one's faults are important parts of fully resolving conflict.

Although Abraham and Abimelech benefited from having further discussions that resolved the remaining issues between them, you should try to resolve all the issues between you and the person you're in conflict with the first time you have a discussion, as issues you leave unresolved may cause serious problems in your life and your relationships. These unresolved issues also may allow Satan and his demon forces to continue to stir up strife and misunderstandings between you and others.

Leaving issues open or not fully resolved also allows people in conflict to repeatedly resurrect these issues against each other. After having discussions, these people may bring up the issue again for more discussion two, three, or even six months later. Some people repeatedly bring up issues for years. In these cases, although they say they want to fully resolve the dispute like Abraham and Abimelech did, this rarely happens. People who do this are very angry, and instead of having fruitful discussions, they repeatedly blame the other person for what he or she has done to cause the conflict to remain. In these situations, there is no closure or full resolution.

Some people revisit these issues because Satan and his demon forces influence them to do this to keep them in conflict. If these demons can cause us to stir up strife with each other every three or six months, Satan has the ability to torment us (and others) and rob us of our rest and peace.

In some cases the people who keep revisiting these issues struggle with bitterness, resentment, and unforgiveness. This is what makes them repeatedly bring up these matters. When these matters are resurrected, the person who is the target suffers great hurt and pain. When these situations arise, he or she commonly says, "I thought this issue was over with. Why does he [or she] keep bringing it up?"

These issues also cause the person to become frustrated and wonder, *When will this end? When will we ever have closure regarding this issue? Will this thing ever die?*

To try to close the door and end repeated revisiting of an issue, pray and ask God to help you get closure. When you're discussing the issue with the person you're in conflict with, you also should do your best to fully discuss the issue so that the conflict is fully resolved.

In some cases you may have to convince the person who wants to revisit things that you won't do this, by saying, "We've already fully discussed this matter, and it's over. We don't need to revisit or rewrite history. You have no good reason to keep bringing up this matter."

If you have a habit of repeatedly revisiting conflict, ask God what causes you to keep revisiting a matter that should be over. You also should repent and let go of the pain and hurt so that you can find peace and move on with your life.

CHAPTER 13

FORGIVE EACH OTHER

For if ye forgive men their trespasses, your heavenly Father will also forgive you: But if ye forgive not men their trespasses, neither will your Father forgive your trespasses.
—Matthew 6:14–15

YOU MAY BE badly hurt and have no desire to forgive the person you're in conflict with because he or she deceived you, betrayed you, or did some terrible wrong to you. Although your pain may be great, I encourage you to fully trust God by opening your heart to be prepared to forgive the person who brought such hurt into your life.

You need to be prepared to forgive the person who hurt you because the Bible instructs you to forgive others as Jesus Christ has forgiven us.

> Let all bitterness, and wrath, and anger, and clamor, and evil speaking be put away from you, with all malice: And be ye kind one to another, tenderhearted, forgiving one another, even as God for Christ's sake hath forgiven you.(Ephesians 4:32)

Preparation for Resolution

Jesus told Peter that we are to walk in continuous forgiveness.

> Then came Peter to him, and said, Lord how oft shall my brother sin against me, and I forgive him? till seven times? Jesus saith unto him, I say not unto thee, Until seven times: but, Until seventy times seven.(Matthew 18:21–22)

I want to share with you a little more about forgiveness so you can understand the concept better. Forgiving a person doesn't mean you become his or her best friend; in fact this doesn't happen in most cases.

Forgiving a person also doesn't mean you agree that what he or she did to you was right or just. If the person robbed, raped, or physically injured you, his or her behavior was wrong.

In addition forgiving a person doesn't mean that you ask the court to set him or her free. It doesn't mean you allow him or her to "get away with murder." People who forgive others often want to hold them accountable for their wrongdoing. But instead of trusting in the penal system or themselves for justice or vengeance, they place the fate of the wrongdoer in God's hands.

> Dearly beloved, avenge not yourselves, but rather give place unto wrath: for it is written, Vengeance is mine; I will repay, saith the Lord.(Romans 12:19)

When you forgive a person, you let go of the malice and ill will you have toward him or her instead of harboring intense anger, bitterness, resentment, hatred, and unforgiveness. According to *Webster's New World Dictionary and Thesaurus*, the word *forgiveness* means to pardon an offense or offender and to give up resentment against the individual or the desire to punish.

Although God instructs you to forgive others, he wants you to do it of your own free will—meaning, he won't force you to do it. However, if you choose not to forgive others, you will suffer some consequences.

Unforgiveness keeps you from being productive and causes you to hurt others.

> Follow peace with all men, and holiness, without which no man shall see the Lord: Looking diligently lest any man fail of the grace of God; lest any root of bitterness springing up trouble you, and thereby many be defiled.(Hebrews 12:14-15)

Not forgiving others also causes you to hurt yourself. An old Chinese proverb warns us that you will hurt yourself by choosing to hold onto resentment: "He who seeks revenge [vengeance] must dig two graves—one for his enemy and one for himself." Life reveals to us that these words are true. People who are bitter and vengeful not only kill others. They stop living the vibrant and fulfilling life that is available to them.

Unforgiveness is sin that separates you from God (see Isaiah 59:1-2); in fact, it causes God not to forgive your sins.

> For if ye forgive men their trespasses, your heavenly Father will also forgive you: But if ye forgive not men their trespasses, neither will your Father forgive your trespasses.(Matthew 6:14-15)

Being unable to forgive also gives the enemy an advantage over you.

> To whom ye forgive anything, I forgive also: for if I forgave anything, to whom I forgave it, for your sakes I forgave it in the person of Christ; Lest Satan should get an advantage of us: for we are not ignorant of his devices.(2 Corinthians 2:10-11)

When you forgive others, you bring the grace and blessings of God alive in your life. As you release the bitterness that binds you, God will heal you and allow you to move forward to fulfill the destiny he has planned for you.

I'm familiar with a number of cases in which family members who were abused or suffered other terrible injustices were able to move forward with powerful, productive lives because they were willing to forgive the person who hurt them. If you want to read some more real-life examples of how God moved in people's lives when they forgave others, I encourage you to read my online article "Encouraging Forgiveness" (see www.mediate.com/mobile/article.cfm?id=3316).

After reading this chapter on forgiveness, some of you probably are thinking, *I want the benefits of forgiveness, but I can't forgive this person for what they've done.* If this is the case, I have a few more words for you.

Let's be honest. All of us have a difficult time forgiving people. God knows this. So he's willing to give you the grace you need to help you forgive others. All you must do is confess your unforgiveness as a sin and ask God for his grace.

Here's a sample prayer you can pray to ask God to help you.

> *Father in heaven, I come to you in need. I know your word says that I should forgive others. But I am holding onto hatred, bitterness, and resentment. I ask that you forgive me for my unforgiveness and bitterness, which are hurting others and myself. I want to be free of this and able to move forward with my life. I ask that you help me release my malice to you so that I may be free of it. Please take away my desire to see this person hurt or to take vengeance against this person. I place my heart in your hands, and I turn this person's life over into your hands. Please give me the grace I need to be able to forgive this person and to move forward. In Jesus' name, amen.*

I'd like to make one final point. In some cases, when you forgive your offender, you free that person from the guilt and shame that imprisons him or her, as Joseph did when he forgave his brothers. About twenty years after Joseph's brothers threw him into a pit and sold him into slavery, they still felt guilty about what they had done.

> And they said one to another, We are very guilty concerning our brother, in that we saw the anguish of his soul, when he

> besought us and we would not hear; therefore is this distress come upon us.(Genesis 42:21)

Joseph's words of forgiveness brought them great deliverance.

> Now therefore be not grieved, nor angry with yourselves, that ye sold me hither; for God did send me before you to preserve life....And God sent me before you to preserve you a posterity in the earth, and to save your lives by a great deliverance.(Genesis 45:5, 7)

If your offender is willing to repent, God may want you to bring deliverance to that individual's life. Are you willing to do this if God asks you?

CHAPTER 14

RECONCILE

Therefore if you bring your gift to the altar, and there remember your brother has something against you, leave your gift before the altar and go your way. First be reconciled to your brother, and then come and offer your gift.
—MATTHEW 5:23–24

WHEN HAVING A discussion with an individual with whom you are in conflict, you should make reconciliation one of your goals because Jesus tells us to reconcile when we know people are upset with us. If God's desire is for us to seek reconciliation, this should be our desire as well.

When the above passage says that you "remember" your brother has something against you, it indicates that the Holy Spirit sometimes prompts us during a time of worship to go and make peace with our brother or sister who is angry with us.

The Bible reveals a number of situations in which God stepped in to woo his people to reconcile with each other. I will share two of them with you. The first involves the conflict between Isaac and Abimelech, the king of the Philistines.

Preparation for Resolution

When Isaac received from God a hundredfold blessing, the Philistines expelled him from their land (Genesis 26:12–17). To get Isaac and the Philistines to talk and make peace, God dealt with the fear in Isaac's heart.

> And the Lord appeared unto him the same night, and said, I am the God of Abraham thy father; fear not, for I am with thee, and will bless thee, and multiply thy seed for my servant Abraham's sake.(Genesis 26:24)

Sometimes fear (fear of bad results, fear of confrontation) keeps us from meeting with each other and trying to resolve our conflicts. Shortly after God addressed Isaac's fear, however, Abimelech went to Isaac and made peace with him.

> And they said, We saw certainly that the Lord was with thee; and we said, Let there be now an oath between us and thee, and let us make covenant with thee.(Genesis 26:28)

The second example is the story of the man whose concubine abandoned him and committed adultery against him.

> And the concubine played the whore against him, and went away from him unto her father's house to Bethlehemjudah, and was there four whole months. (Judges 19:2)

When people leave us like this, their ever returning to us may look impossible. But instead of giving up hope, this man went to his father-in-law's house to reclaim his bride.

> And her husband arose, and went after her, to speak friendly unto her, and to bring her again. (Judges 19:3)

When the man went to get his bride, God met him. God moved her heart so she would reconcile with her husband, and they planned to go back home together.

> And when the man rose up to depart, he, and his concubine, and his servant, his father-in-law, the damsel's father, said unto him, Behold, now the day draweth toward evening, I pray you tarry all night: behold, the day groweth to an end, lodge here, that thine heart may be merry; and tomorrow get you early on your way, that thou mayest go home.(Judges 19:9)

Today God makes this kind of reconciliation available to couples who offer their hearts to God.

In addition to these biblical examples, I want to share three other real-life cases where God moved people's hearts to try to get them to talk and reconcile.

One situation involved a member of our congregation who sought my prayer and counsel while trying to deal with the terrible conflict that divided her family. About a month after she sought help, God healed a child in the family who was near and dear to everyone involved in the disagreement. When this happened, God moved the hearts of the people in conflict, and they began to talk after a long period of not speaking to each other. A few other times I have seen God physically heal someone in conflict (or their relative or close friend), and the healing influenced the people in conflict to start discussions with each other.

The second situation involved a dispute between my aunt and uncle over some property. The two of them went to court against each other, and they stopped speaking to each other for a number of years. Then, one Christmas, I witnessed a powerful miracle take place in which they came together and reconciled at my uncle's house. Their tears and embracing each other showed how real the reconnection between them was. After years of not communicating, they regularly talked to each other until my aunt died. When I think about what God did in this situation, I realize that we serve a powerful, awesome God.

The third situation involved some clients of mine who were going through severe marital difficulties, and they agreed to fill out papers to get a divorce. On the day before they planned to go to the courthouse, the husband decided to call me. He had no idea if I was a divorce lawyer or if I could help him. He felt that he could trust me because of the relationship we had built when I handled another case for him.

When he called me, he said to me, "We're having problems, and I thought about you. We have nowhere to go. Maybe you can help us?" I agreed to meet with them to see if there was anything I could do.

When the couple came to see me, I could feel the tension, hopeless and pain. But as I asked them questions about what they thought about each other and whether they loved each other, the atmosphere began to change. By their words, you could tell they still loved each other. When they both came to the understanding that they really wanted to stay together, they agreed to start attending church and marital counseling together instead of going to divorce court. When this couple left my office with smiles on their faces and renewed hope, I knew that this had not come about because of any skills or ability I had. God was the one who inspired this husband to call me. In addition, God moved their hearts to convince them to continue to work at saving their marriage.

Just as God stepped in to help Isaac and Abimelech and the others I mentioned in my examples, he will move our hearts to try to persuade those of us in conflict to reconcile with each other.

When we seek reconciliation, *we ask God to restore our damaged or destroyed relationship.* Matthew 18:15 refers to reconciliation as "gaining our brother."

> Moreover if your brother sins against you, go and tell him his fault between you and him alone. If he hears you, you have gained your brother.

A very important point must be made here. For reconciliation to occur, it takes two people who are willing to yield to God and meet his conditions. Many of us, however, do not want to reconcile because the person who hurt us has offended us, and we do not want to salvage the relationship because of what he or she has done to us.

> A brother offended is harder to be won than a strong city: and their contentions are like the bars of a castle. (Proverbs 18:19)

This truth is reflected in the words that people in conflict commonly say when I mention the subject of reconciliation: "I want him to repay me what he owes me, and then I want nothing more to do with him."

Many people in conflict whom I've encountered are totally against reconciliation. I'm not denying how terrible the hurt is in many of these situations. Life and my experience as a mediator have taught me that we can be inhumane and do very cruel things to each other.

But God wants us to open our hearts to the possibility of reconciliation instead of having hardened hearts that are totally closed to reconciliation. When Jesus spoke about divorce in Matthew 19:7–8, his words revealed the following:

> They say unto him, Why did Moses then command to give a writing of divorcement, and to put her away? He saith unto them, Moses because of the hardness of your hearts suffered you to put away your wives: but from the beginning it was not so.

Jesus was saying that some people who sever their relationships by getting divorces do so because their hearts are hardened, and they're unwilling to forgive each other. In some instances people who have gotten divorced could have saved their marriages if they had opened their hearts to God and experienced a mighty move of his spirit in their lives.

If you lack the desire to reconcile, go to the altar and repent for any unforgiveness, resentment, and hatred you're holding in your heart against the person with whom you're in conflict. You may be deeply hurt, but in God's eyes, holding onto intense anger or bitterness is never justified.

Hebrews 12:14–15 speaks about having a root of bitterness:

Preparation for Resolution

> Follow peace with all men, and holiness, without which no man shall see the Lord: Looking diligently lest any fail of the grace of God; lest any root of bitterness springing up trouble you, and thereby many be defiled.

According to these verses, having a root of bitterness "defiles many." If you feel bitter, repent of your bitterness to end the pain that those who are near and dear to you may be suffering because of you. You also may need to ask God to give you his grace to make reconciliation possible.

If you truly want reconciliation, you also must open your heart to allow God to change you. In Matthew 5:24, the Greek word for *reconcile* is *diallaso*, which, according to *Strong's Concordance*, means to change thoroughly.

This word indicates that God will do a deep, powerful work of transformation in you and your relationships when the people in conflict are willing to work together as God leads them through a process in which he knits their hearts back together. When people in conflict fully cooperate with God and work together, their relationship often ends up healthier and stronger than ever.

Earlier in the book, I mentioned how God did a powerful work in my father's life to free him of the anger that afflicted him and also allowed us to reconcile. This work didn't happen in one day. It took place little by little over time as we yielded to the leading of the Holy Spirit.

I'm starting to see more cases in which the Holy Spirit is entering people's hearts, causing them to turn to God and allow him to reconcile them with each other.

> And he shall turn the hearts of the fathers to the children, and the hearts of the children to the fathers.(Malachi 4:6)

The process of reconciliation may take awhile because it often takes a long time to restore trust and love when people in conflict have deeply hurt each other. Some individuals may need someone from their church's ministry staff to help guide them through the process of reconciliation when others have abused or terribly wounded them.

At this point I encourage you to go before God and yield to the Holy Spirit as he moves your heart to seek reconciliation with those with whom you are in conflict.

Conclusion

I hope that this book has given you the insight you need and that you are taking the required steps to be fully prepared to meet and resolve your conflict. In closing I'd like to share two more Scriptures to remind you how mighty God is so that you can trust him to help you resolve your differences with others.

> *Come behold the works of the Lord, who has made desolations in the earth. He maketh wars to cease unto the ends of the earth; He breaks the bow and cuts the spear in two. He burns the chariots in the fire.*
> —Psalm 46:9

> *And he shall judge among the nations, and shall rebuke many people: and they shall beat their swords into plowshares, and their spears into pruninghooks: nation shall not lift up sword against nation, neither shall they learn war again.*
> —Isaiah 2:4

Resources

Please consult the following resources if you need more help to prepare to resolve your conflict.

God's Power Released, Lester L. Adams, 2013. This handbook provides congregation members insight into obedience to God's word, which releases God's power to resolve conflict (available at www.amazon.com/dp/B00C7TCWJE).

"The Four Questions of Anger," Lester L. Adams (www.mediate.com/articles/adamsL11.cfm). This article helps us address and resolve destructive anger in our lives.

"Praying People and Conflict Resolution," Lester L. Adams (www.mediate.com/articles/adamsL10.cfm). This article gives insight into praying scripturally based prayers that prepare our hearts to resolve our differences with others.

"Congregational Conflict Resolution and the Use of Scriptures," Lester L. Adams (www.mediate.com/articles/adamsl2.cfm). This article provides insight into how to use God's word to resolve conflict.

About The Author

Lester Adams is a lawyer, mediator, author and ordained minister who has a passion to see God bring reconciliation, peace, and unity into our lives. In 1994, while Lester was praying and seeking God's will for his life, God gave him a prophetic word indicating that there would be a major change in the direction of his life and ministry.

Lester had heard of the terms "mediation" and "reconciliation," but he had no idea what they meant. In this prophetic word, God revealed to Lester that he would begin to offer God's ministry of mediation and reconciliation "to a world of people who need it desperately."

God also promised to give Lester "new knowledge" and great joy and fulfillment in providing people this ministry because this was the will of God for his life.

Over the past twenty years, God has been fulfilling the word that he gave to Lester. God has given him new knowledge of himself as the Prince of Peace, who makes his peace to resolve conflict available to us as we surrender to him and obey his word.

God has also opened up doors for Lester to mediate conflicts, and to teach individuals, families, congregations, and organizations how to use the scriptures to resolve conflict.

The "great joy" and "fulfillment" prophesied has also happened. God's word is like a "fire shut up" in Lester's bones (See Jeremiah 20: 9). In addition, it greatly pleases Lester when God gives him the opportunity to preach God's word to people or a congregation, and to see God move to resolve conflict and to set people free.

Offering the ministry to a "world of people" started to occur when Lester started writing articles on congregational conflict resolution. These articles have been read and disseminated throughout the United States and in places as far away as Israel, India, Spain, Germany, the Philippines, Botswana, and Zimbabwe.

In the last few years, God has inspired Lester to write and publish books to declare and reveal God's power to help equip people to more effectively use the scriptures to resolve their conflict with each other. These books give Biblical and real life examples (from his life and his experience as a mediator, lawyer and ordained minister) to reveal how God is able to help us resolve our disagreements. It is Lester's hope that God continues to expand the borders of his ministry so that more people throughout the world will be able to receive the peace, mediation, and reconciliation that God offers us.

www.ingramcontent.com/pod-product-compliance
Lightning Source LLC
Chambersburg PA
CBHW060356050426
42449CB00009B/1759